Popular Culture:
1900–1919

Jilly Hunt

Heinemann
LIBRARY

Chicago, Illinois

www.capstonepub.com
Visit our website to find out more information about Heinemann-Raintree books.

To order:

☎ Phone 800-747-4992

📖 Visit www.capstonepub.com to browse our catalog and order online.

Edited by Adam Miller, Andrew Farrow, and Adrian Vigliano
Designed by Richard Parker
Original illustrations © Capstone Global Ltd 2012
Illustrations by Richard Parker
Picture research by Mica Brancic
Originated by Capstone Global Library Ltd
Printed and bound in China by Leo Paper Products Ltd

16 15 14 13 12
10 9 8 7 6 5 4 3 2 1

Library of Congress Cataloging-in-Publication Data
Hunt, Jilly.
 Popular culture : 1900-1919 / Jilly Hunt.
 p. cm.—(A history of popular culture)
 Includes bibliographical references and index.
 ISBN 978-1-4109-4621-8 (hb)—ISBN 978-1-4109-4628-7 (pb) 1. Popular culture—United States—History—20th century—Juvenile literature. 2. United States—Civilization—1865-1918—Juvenile literature. 3. United States—Social life and customs—1865-1918—Juvenile literature. I. Title. II. Title: 1900-1919.
 E168.H896 2013
 973.91—dc23   2011038399

973.91
Hunt

Acknowledgments
We would like to thank the following for permission to reproduce photographs: Alamy p. 25 (© Lebrecht Music and Arts Photo Library); Art Archive p. 34 (The Owen Trust); Corbis pp. 18 (© Bettmann), 37 (© Robert Landau); Getty Images pp. 15 (Archive Photos/Buyenlarge), 31, 33, 42 (Archive Photos/Buyenlarge), 29 (Buyenlarge), 38 (Frank Lloyd Wright Preservation Trust), 17 (Gamma-Keystone), 21, 30 (Gamma-Keystone/Keystone-France), 26, 45 (Hulton Archive), 7, 13 (Hulton Archive/Apic), 27 (Hulton Archive/Central Press), 6, 49, 51 (Hulton Archive/Topical Press Agency), 5 (Hulton Archive/Topical Press Agency/A. R. Coster), 52 (Popperfoto/Bob Thomas), 35 (Popperfoto/Paul Popper), 11 (Science & Society Picture Library), 53 (Sean Gallup), 9 (Sean Sexton), 23 (Redferns/GAB Archive); Library of Congress pp. 41 [Lewis Hine/Photographs from the records of the National Child Labor Committee (U.S)], 46 (Prints and Photographs Division); Mary Evans Picture Library p. 43 (Onslow Auctions Limited); Photoshot p. 39 (© UPPA); The Kobal Collection p. 16 (EDISON). Background images and design features reproduced with permission of Shutterstock.

Cover photograph of four women laughing while running on a beach reproduced with the permission of Getty Images (Harold M. Lambert).

Every effort has been made to contact copyright holders of any material reproduced in this book. Any omissions will be rectified in subsequent printings if notice is given to the publisher.

Disclaimer
All the Internet addresses (URLs) given in this book were valid at the time of going to press. However, due to the dynamic nature of the Internet, some addresses may have changed, or sites may have changed or ceased to exist since publication. While the author and publisher regret any inconvenience this may cause readers, no responsibility for any such changes can be accepted by either the author or the publisher.

Contents

Some words are printed in bold, **like this**. You can find out what they mean by looking in the glossary.

What Is Popular Culture?

What do you enjoy doing in your free time? Do you enjoy watching a movie or some television? Or perhaps you like reading a good book or flipping through the pages of a magazine to find out about the latest fashions? Chances are that a lot of other people like the same movies, television programs, books, or magazines as you. This makes these pastimes part of a popular culture.

The word *culture* can be used in many ways, but in this book we mean culture to be the arts, such as movies, music, books, and design. Culture can also include elements that are part of everyday life such as travel and the clothes people wear.

Popular culture really came into being with the introduction of mass communication such as television and radio. In the years between 1900 and 1919, mass communication was just beginning. This was an exciting time of inventions and technological advances. Can you imagine a world without television? Well that was our world during this time. Television wasn't widely introduced until the 1920s. Going to a movie theater was a new experience in the early 1900s, since movies were only available to the general public in about 1896.[1] Can you imagine what it would have been like to see your first "moving picture," as they were called then, projected onto a big screen?

Where does popular culture start?

Popular culture might vary in different countries or there might be trends that appeal to lots of people around the world.

Sometimes an advance in technology means that an item, such as the car, will become more affordable. This will have an impact on how people live their lives. A new car means that traveling to see friends or relatives may become a lot easier. Many new cars on the road may also mean traffic jams and an increase in pollution.

Sometimes trends, such as designer fashion, start with the elite. A new look is then adapted to make it accessible and affordable to the mainstream public. The reverse of this might also happen. A trend might start with a particular subgroup of people and spread to become widely popular. For example, ragtime and jazz developed within the African American community. During the early 1900s, racism among the wealthy, social elite (and throughout

society) caused people to view blacks and their culture as taboo. However, ragtime and jazz soared to popularity among the elite and other groups.

The appeal of movie theaters spread around the world, and they became a key part of popular culture. This crowd is waiting to enter a "kinema" (an old spelling of "cinema") in London, England, in 1918.

What was the world like in the 1900s and 1910s?

The twentieth century started out with Britain being the most powerful nation in the world. But by 1919 the world had become a very different place. **World War I** (1914–1918) was on a scale not seen before.

Age of imperialism

At the turn of the century, the British **Empire** was at its height. This was the age of **imperialism**. Great Britain, under the rule of Queen Victoria, had many colonies around the world, including India, Canada, New Zealand, Australia, and South Africa. This meant Great Britain was a strong global influence. What was popular in the United Kingdom would be spread around the world to its colonies.

These British soliders are returning home from fighting in World War I in 1915.

Around this time, the global influence of the United States began to strengthen. It was the beginning of the "American Century," in which American manufacturing power would overtake the European industrial powers and empires of the United Kingdom, Germany, and France.

World War I

The big event that affected people all over the world was World War I (1914–1918). About 8.5 million people were killed and more than 21 million wounded.[2] It was the first industrial war, though people had thought that new technologies would stop wars. Instead, technological advances and mass production made World War I one of the most brutal and horrific wars the world had ever seen. The war changed the way people thought. The social restrictions in place before the war now seemed less important. When people were dying, what did it matter what style of jacket one wore to a formal dinner? The general public wanted to be freer from these restrictions, and this was displayed in various ways: from the way people dressed to the kind of music they enjoyed.

Fight for the right to vote

Women around the world had been fighting for their right to vote since the nineteenth century, particularly in the United States and United Kingdom. However, other countries gave women the right to vote earlier than the United States and United Kingdom did. For example, New Zealand granted the right in 1893, Australia in 1902, Finland in 1906, and Norway in 1913.[3]

Campaigners for women's rights would often hold demonstrations and perform militant actions in order to draw attention to their plight. In the United Kingdom, campaigners chained themselves to railings, refused to pay taxes, and went on hunger strike if they were imprisoned. One **suffragette**, Emily Davidson, died after she threw herself under the king's horse.[4]

Bicycles became a symbol of new freedom and rights for women (see page 47).

World War I sped up the **franchise** of women, because while men were away fighting, women did many of the jobs that the men had left.

Time to travel

This was an exciting time for technical advances in transportation. Previously travel had only been for the very rich, but transportation was becoming more affordable. In the late nineteenth century the main way to travel was by horse and cart or horse-drawn carriages.[5] As the twentieth century progressed the options for travel increased. Public transportation also grew with the opening of subway systems in cities around the world. Train travel became more accessible as the rail networks in the United States and Europe neared completion. Ocean travel became faster and people were taking to the air in the first planes.

These developments in travel also influenced popular culture, especially for the middle classes. An increase in prosperity meant that people had more time available for leisure activities, including going on vacations. The railways made it possible for people to travel larger distances in a shorter time. Seaside vacations, if only for a day, became very popular, especially in the United Kingdom.

Sinking of the unsinkable

The *Titanic* was hailed by its owner, White Star Line, as being unsinkable. However, on its first voyage across the Atlantic Ocean in April 1912, the *Titanic* hit an iceberg and sank, killing around 1,490 people. This tragic loss of life led to new regulations about the number of lifeboats ships would carry. The events of the *Titanic* have inspired numerous stories, movies, songs, and works of art, and the story continues to fascinate people today.

Traveling trends

The accessibility to travel meant that popular trends spread farther and more quickly. For example, the expanding train system and the riverboats of the Mississippi River helped the popularity of ragtime and early jazz spread up from New Orleans, Louisiana, in the south to the northern cities of the United States.[6]

Traveling for work

The subway system developed at the turn of the century. These railway systems linked urban and suburban areas, providing faster travel and allowing people to commute into city centers for work or leisure. London had the first underground train line, which opened in 1863 using steam locomotives.[7] London's first electric underground train was in service in 1890, and more lines were electrified through the early 1900s.[8] Cities around the world started developing subways: Budapest's subway opened in 1896, Paris's Metro in 1900, Boston's subway in 1897, New York City's subway in 1904, and Philadelphia's in 1907.[9]

The improving railway network allowed people to travel farther in a shorter period of time. People were able to visit places, like the ocean, just for the day.

CORK TRALEE

Air travel takes off

The desire to fly has been around for centuries, but in 1903 Orville and Wilbur Wright made the first successful engine-powered, heavier-than-air flight carrying a person.[10] On June 14 to 15, 1919, John Alcock and Arthur Whitten Brown made the first nonstop Atlantic flight. It took 16 hours and 27 minutes from Newfoundland, Canada, to Clifden, Ireland.[11] Aircraft were used in World War I, but it wasn't until the second half of the twentieth century that **commercial flights** were inexpensive enough to be a travel option.

Impact of the car

The rich were traditionally the only people who could afford private transportation up until the late nineteenth century. In the first few decades of the twentieth century this was beginning to change. In 1903, the Ford Motor Company sold its first cars.[12] In 1908, Ford released the Model T, and it proved so popular that Henry Ford had to think about ways he could produce the car in large quantities but at low cost. In 1913, Ford opened the first moving **assembly line** in Michigan.[13] This revolutionized manufacturing techniques of all kinds of goods, not just cars. Goods could now be made more cheaply, and therefore would be more affordable to the masses.

Initially cars weren't very popular to the everyday person. They were seen as noisy and dangerous. In Britain, the 1903 Motor Car Act set a top speed of 20 miles per hour (32 kilometers per hour), which seems very slow compared to today's speeds.

But the car changed society. It made people more mobile and gave them the freedom to go where they wanted. It created the need for roads and changed the appearance of towns and cities. It allowed people to live farther away from their jobs and drive to them. Ford's idea of turning the car from a luxury into an everyday essential by making it cheap enough for many people to afford was realized.[14]

Travel as immigrants

Popular culture was also spread by the increase in immigration around the world. In 1901, the Australian government encouraged British **emigrants** to Australia by offering land.[15] In the early twentieth century,[16] large numbers of European **immigrants** came to the United States. Over 2 million Italians, 1.5 million Jews, and 0.5 million Slavs[17] immigrated to the United States looking to escape economic and religious persecution. Many of the poorer immigrants were not educated and could not speak the language of their new country. They often had to take the low-paying jobs offered by expanding industries. But they contributed to the culture of the United States and added to it with their own forms of popular culture. For example, there was a strong Jewish theater and **vaudeville** scene (see pages 20-21).

Ford's Model T became hugely popular. Only one paint, Japan black enamel, would dry fast enough to cope with the speed of the production line so customers could have "any color they want so long as it's black."

Assembly lines

Assembly lines are set up so that a worker performs a specific task. An assembly line building a car starts with a bare chassis. Then the different components are added by the workers along the line in a specific order. This method speeds up production because each worker does only one specific task, has the equipment needed for that task, and becomes skilled at doing it.

Children's Entertainment

At first the world of children's entertainment in the 1900s and 1910s might seem very different to you because there were no computer games or television. Instantly recognizable characters such as Buzz Lightyear and Spider-Man didn't exist. However, you are probably also very familiar with some of the popular toys from these decades.

Jigsaw puzzles have been around since the eighteenth century, but it wasn't until the 1860s and 1870s that popular pictures were used as jigsaws in the United States and United Kingdom. These puzzles became extremely popular in the early 1900s.[1]

Did you know?

The teddy bear was named after U.S. president Theodore Roosevelt. While on a hunting trip in 1902, Roosevelt refused to shoot a bear cub. This inspired a toy maker to name a stuffed bear after him—his nickname was Teddy. The craze for teddy bears began![2]

Have you ever created a picture using wax crayons? In 1903, Crayola crayons were made by Edwin Binney and C. Harold Smith.[3]

The Meccano set, or Erector set, was invented by Frank Hornby in Liverpool, England, in 1901.[4] This was a construction set consisting of a variety of reusable parts such as metal strips, plates, wheels, **axles**, and gears, along with nuts and bolts to connect it all together. The users could build working models and mechanical devices and be like real engineers. These sets are still available to buy today.

A much loved possession, this boy gives his teddy bear a cuddle in 1906.

CULTURE IN CONTEXT

At the beginning of the twentieth century it was still common for children from working-class families to have to go to work, often in factories, shipbuilding yards, or in mines. The 1900 U.S. census showed that about two million children were employed.[5] **Child labor** was also common in the United Kingdom at this time, but the introduction of compulsory education helped reduce the number of child laborers. It wasn't until 1918 that compulsory education became law in every state in the United States.[6] There would be little time for play for some working-class children.

Film and Light Entertainment

Going to the movies became a hugely popular form of entertainment in the first few decades of the twentieth century. Motion pictures had a big impact on popular culture, with people following the careers of their favorite stars and wanting to look like them. Going to the movies wasn't expensive, so it was accessible to a large part of the population.

Early beginnings

Motion pictures became available to the general public around 1896. At first, the short films were shown as part of music hall shows, also called vaudeville (see pages 18-19), or circus shows. In 1902 in Los Angeles, California, a shop opened that showed only moving pictures and was a great success. This led to the opening of movie houses throughout the United States. In Pittsburgh, Pennsylvania, in 1905 the first movie theater was opened. It cost a nickel to get in so it became known as the nickelodeon.[1] The first nickelodeons appealed to the working class but gradually became popular with the middle class as well.

Did you know?

In the United States in 1905, there were only a few permanent movie theaters. By 1908, there were between 8,000 and 10,000.[2]

The early film industry

Up until 1914, the film industry was international and led by the United States, France, Britain, and Italy. European movies were dominated by Charles Pathé and his brother.[3] Their company commissioned its own studio camera, which was better than other cameras. They also built a production facility in France where movies could be made using an assembly line approach.[4]

But World War I changed things. There was an increased demand for films, because people wanted to escape the reality of everyday life. But with the Europeans at war, they couldn't meet this demand. The United States took the lead and became the foremost filmmaking country in the world. Perhaps when you think of U.S. filmmaking you think of Hollywood, California. However, the first U.S. studios were in New York City or Chicago, Illinois, because of the pool of theater actors available in those cities.

An advertisement for a motion picture from the 1900s based on Edgar Allen Poe's *The Raven*.

A move to warmer climates

It was the high demand for films that led to the film industry's move to Hollywood. Film companies needed to be able to film year-round. Since most movies were shot outdoors in available light, the winter conditions in New York and Chicago weren't ideal. The film industry needed to move to a warmer climate with clearer skies. They needed a new center, and a suburb of Los Angeles called Hollywood proved to be just the place.

Silent movies

Early movies were very different from the movies we are used to today. They were short, silent comedies, dramas, or documentaries. Music would be played, usually by a live pianist in front of the screen. The actors would not speak. In between scenes, **title cards** appeared on-screen explaining what was happening or providing **dialogue**.

Initially movies were only a few minutes long—more like today's commercials. In 1903, Edwin S. Porter revolutionized filmmaking by editing the movie to tell a story in different locations. His 1903 movie *Life of an American Fireman*[5] was the first U.S. documentary movie and contained film of actual fire scenes combined with actors playing the role of fire chief–hero and a trapped mother and child. He created the feeling of suspense by cutting back and forth between the frightened mother and the brave firefighters.

The first blockbuster

D. W. Griffith's 1915 silent movie *The Birth of a Nation*[6] is considered the first Hollywood blockbuster. It was the most profitable movie of its time. The film is about the American Civil War (1861–1865) and was admired for its technical and dramatic innovations, but was condemned for the racism contained within its story. The movie cost $100,000[7] to make, which was a lot of money at the time, but it was so successful that it made millions of dollars in profit.[8] *The Birth of a Nation* showed the power and popularity of movies and that going to movies was now a middle-class pastime. It was clear that there was money to be made in the film industry.

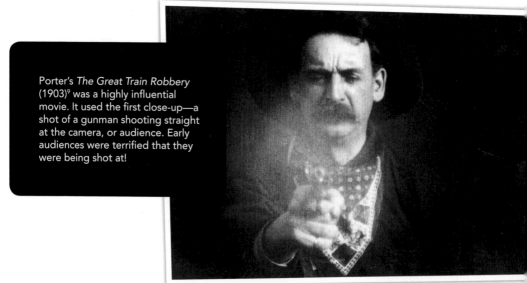

Porter's *The Great Train Robbery* (1903)[9] was a highly influential movie. It used the first close-up—a shot of a gunman shooting straight at the camera, or audience. Early audiences were terrified that they were being shot at!

Fluctuation in movie audience numbers in the United Kingdom[10]

Year	Number of viewers
1916	20 million
1946	1.6 billion
1956	1.1 billion
1960	501 million

Charlie Chaplin was one of the stars of the silent movies.

The star system

Today we are all very familiar with the names of big movie stars. However, it wasn't always this way. In 1909,[11] movie producer Carl Laemmle introduced the star system to the United States by promoting actress Florence Lawrence. Before this, actors were not known by name. For example, the actress Mary Pickford, who became one of the richest and most famous women in the United States, was initially known only as the "Biograph Girl with the Curls."[12] Other movie studios saw that promoting actors and actresses could improve business, so they started distributing **publicity stills**. The star system was born and has developed into the multimillion dollar global business that it is today.

Animation

In 1906, the first animated cartoon was produced by J. Stuart Blackton. It was called *Humorous Phases of Funny Faces*. Other animators followed suit, such as Winsor McCay with *Gertie the Dinosaur*. The first star of **animation** was probably Felix the Cat, created by Otto Messmer in 1919.[13]

Music hall and vaudeville

The movies started as part of the entertainment in shows called vaudeville, as they were known in the United States, or music hall in the United Kingdom. These were a kind of **variety show**. Both shows were a similar form of light entertainment. They included a series of individual acts featuring singers, dancers, jugglers, magicians, acrobats, comedians, and trained animals.

A vaudeville performance in progress.

Origins

In the United States, vaudeville started in the 1850s and 1860s in beer halls and was aimed mainly at men. By the late nineteenth century it had become more respectable, was held in theaters, and was considered family entertainment. Music hall in the United Kingdom came from the working-class concerts given in pubs during the eighteenth and nineteenth centuries. Eventually this style of entertainment moved to music clubs, saloons, and concert halls. Vaudeville was the height of fashion in entertainment from about the mid-1890s to the early 1930s.

Future stars

Vaudeville and music hall made stars of many performers. W. C. Fields was an American juggler and comedian. He appeared in vaudeville and in *Ziegfeld Follies* **revues** between 1915 and 1921, before he became established in films and thereby an internationally famous comic.[15]

Harry Houdini, the great escape artist, took part in vaudeville shows as a trapeze artist, but he wasn't very successful. It was his daring escape attempts while shackled with ropes, chains, and handcuffs and submerged underwater or suspended upside down high above the ground that gained him an international reputation.

Buster Keaton, who became a silent film star, began performing in vaudeville acts when he was just three years old. His parents were also vaudeville performers who specialized in a type of acrobatics called knockabout. His father used Buster as a "human mop."[16]

The end of vaudeville

The huge popularity of motion pictures gradually edged out vaudeville. Movies started to dominate the shows, and by about 1927 the shows consisted mostly of full-length motion pictures with added vaudeville acts.[17]

Ziegfeld's revues

Florenz Ziegfeld was an American theatrical producer who made a big impact with his revues, starting in 1907.[14] His slogan was "Glorifying the American Girl." These shows featured seminudity, **pageantry**, and comedy. The *Ziegfeld Follies* were based on the Folies Bergère of Paris but were less **risqué**. (The Folies Bergère was a Parisian music hall famed for its displays of female nudity.) Ziegfeld developed stars such as singer and comedienne Fanny Brice, and comedians Eddie Cantor, Will Rogers, and Bert Williams.

Jewish influence

At the turn of the century, the United States was the destination of many of Europe's emigrants. There were large numbers of Italians, Slavs, and Jews leaving Europe in the hope of escaping poverty and persecution and living the American dream of freedom and opportunity. The different nationalities brought with them their own cultures, which influenced the popular culture of the areas they settled in. Many Jewish immigrants settled in America's northeast, in cities such as New York and Boston. In the big cities the popular forms of entertainment such as vaudeville and theater were well established but the film industry was still growing. Jewish immigrants got involved in all forms of the entertainment industry and heavily influenced popular culture.

Many Jewish performers became part of American vaudeville, including such big-name stars as Fanny Brice, Eddie Cantor, and Al Jolson. A separate circuit of vaudeville, called Yiddish vaudeville, was named after the Yiddish language spoken by many of the eastern European Jews.

Anti-Semitism
During this time there were a lot of negative feelings toward Jews and they were often persecuted. This is called **anti-Semitism**. Many of the Jewish performers of vaudeville made their religion the main part of their act in a humorous way. This helped bring a greater understanding of the Jewish culture to the audience and helped to soften anti-Semitic attitudes.

The move to Hollywood
It was a natural move for many of these performers to go to Hollywood when the film industry relocated there. For example, theater and screen actor Paul Muni achieved great success in Hollywood. His reputation as a stage actor meant that Hollywood couldn't stereotype him into certain roles, so he had the rare luxury of approving the scripts of the movies he worked on.[18]

Many Jewish immigrants, such as filmmaker and producer Samuel Goldwyn and motion picture executive Louis B. Mayer, were involved behind the scenes in the Hollywood film industry. Together with Marcus Loew, who owned Metro Pictures, they formed the company Metro-Goldwyn-Mayer, or MGM, which is still a big name in the film industry today.[19]

Al Jolson (1886-1950)

Al Jolson was born in Russia in 1886 but lived in the United States from the age of seven. He made his first stage appearance in 1899 in a vaudeville act with his brother. Jolson became a popular New York entertainer and singer. In 1927, he starred in *The Jazz Singer*, which was the first feature film to have **synchronized** speech. The film is about a boy struggling to balance Jewish life with his love of performing.

Music

The early 1900s was an exciting time for music. Famous writers and performers, such as composers Claude Debussy, Gustav Mahler, Richard Strauss, Igor Stravinsky, and opera singers Caruso and Nelly Melba, were busy creating and entertaining. But there were talented musicians who couldn't make it in this musical world because of the color of their skin. African Americans were treated as second-class citizens and weren't permitted to take part in or contribute to the white music of high society. African American musicians formed their own musical styles with ragtime, blues, and jazz. These styles would soon have a big influence around the world.

Ragtime music

Ragtime was an incredibly popular form of music in the United States from 1899 to 1917.[1] It was the forerunner of jazz. Ragtime emerged from various forms of African American music and was influenced by folk and brass band music, as well as black and white minstrel shows (see box on page 24).

The main instrument in ragtime music is the piano. Ragtime is a style of playing based on **honky-tonk** piano playing. In ragtime, the right-hand beat is syncopated, which means the strong beat gets weaker and the weak beat gets stronger. The fresh rhythms and smooth sounds of ragtime appealed to millions of Americans.

Ragtime on paper

By the turn of the century, ragtime music began to be published. The first "rag" published was called "Harlem Rag" and was by Tom Turpin.[2] Easy-to-read versions of ragtime music were published for people to play on their pianos at home. As the leisure time of middle-class Americans increased, so did the demand for sheet music. The piano was a popular addition in the parlor of many American homes. It served as a form of entertainment and also a status symbol.[3] Ragtime was an African American music form that transferred easily to the white mainstream because it was instrumental. Scott Joplin was a popular ragtime composer whose music sold in the thousands.

Did you know?

Scott Joplin's "Maple Leaf Rag" was published in 1899 and sold 75,000 copies in the first year.[4]

Scott Joplin became one of the first African Americans to enjoy widespread fame.

Scott Joplin (1868-1917)

Scott Joplin was a talented American pianist and composer. He taught himself to play the piano before getting formal lessons at the age of eleven.[5] Joplin was a leading figure in ragtime and was known as the King of Ragtime. He was one of the first ragtime musicians to write down the music. His hits included "Maple Leaf Rag," "Swipesy Cakewalk," and "The Entertainer." He died in 1917. Joplin's popularity and that of ragtime were revived in the 1970s when "The Entertainer" was used in a very popular movie, *The Sting*.

Early jazz

Ragtime developed before jazz and continued to be popular along with early jazz. Some ragtime musicians were involved in the creation of early jazz. But jazz took off in a big way and has been a major influence on popular culture around the world ever since.

Jazz developed in the southern United States in the early twentieth century. Like ragtime, it started with African American musicians and its appeal quickly spread to a large section of society. It was the popular music to listen to and dance to in bars and saloons, and it remains popular today.

What is jazz?

Jazz is an informal sound that often utilizes up-tempo rhythms. It is a combination of West African rhythms with elements from ragtime, brass bands, blues, and **work songs**. The work songs that influenced jazz are the songs sung by African American slaves and workers to relieve the boredom of a repetitive task. They were often spiritual in nature.

Brass band music, particularly that of New Orleans marching bands, is an important part of jazz. Brass bands would play for a variety of functions, but mostly for funerals. On the way to the burial the band would play mournful music known as a dirge. On the way back, they would play happy, faster music. These bands would play **improvised** tunes, which is a key element in jazz. The musicians did not play from written sheet music. Instead, each musician played the tune in a different way. Some of jazz's legendary figures, such as Buddy Bolden and King Oliver, were involved in these marching bands.

CULTURE IN CONTEXT: Black and white minstrel show

Minstrel shows were traveling bands of entertainers who performed songs and music of African American origin. These bands are now controversial because the performers were white people with their faces blackened by makeup in order to appear African American. The humor, based on racial stereotypes, is now considered offensive.

King Oliver (with trumpet, back row) was a leading figure in early jazz. He was also the person who saw the talent and potential in the young musician Louis Armstrong (kneeling, center). Armstrong became one of the most famous jazz trumpeters ever.

Birth of the blues

The blues emerged at the same time as jazz, and the two music forms influenced each other. Like jazz, the blues developed in the southern United States by African American musicians at the turn of the century. Blues musicians mixed work songs with African and white folk music. The first blues **record** was published in 1912. It was called "Memphis Blues" and was by W. C. Handy.[6]

Dance

In the early twentieth century, some Americans were looking for new dances. As ragtime music became more acceptable, high society ballrooms started to do the cakewalk. This dance involved couples forming a square, with men on the inside. The couples then strutted around the square to the music. Judges evaluated the dancers based on their elegance, grace, and inventiveness, gradually eliminating the couples who were not the best dancers. The winning couple was presented with a cake.[7] Scott Joplin's "Swipesy Cakewalk" was a popular tune for this dance.

Dancers performing the cakewalk at the Pan Am Expo in Buffalo, New York, in 1901.

The dances performed to ragtime were mainly the one-step. This is where a couple walked one step to each beat of the music. Its simplicity was part of its popularity because everyone could do it. Those who were more skilled in dance could also choose from the Argentine tango, the hesitation waltz, the Brazilian maxixe, or the fox-trot.

In Europe, the younger generation embraced the more lively, exciting dances coming from the United States. They took up the the one-step, two-step, the turkey trot, the fox-trot, and the quickstep.[8]

A gramophone is being used to attract attention to a recruitment drive in London for World War I soldiers.

The music business

In the early twentieth century, the music industry was very different from how it is now. The most common way for people to buy music was as sheet music so that they could play the tune themselves. A popular social activity was gathering at someone's home and singing songs around a piano.

People had been experimenting with different ways of recording and playing back sounds and music since the mid-1850s.[9] But it wasn't until 1887 that the record was invented. These records were flat disks that held sound grooves in a spiral. They could be played back on a gramophone. By 1915, the 78 **rpm (revolutions per minute)** record had been introduced and it allowed a playing time of about four and a half minutes per side, which was enough for one or two songs per side.

Improvements in recording and playback technology allowed people to reproduce music on a larger scale for the general public. Recorded music and sheet music sales prospered as people had more and more free time. The pleasure and escapism provided by popular music was especially in demand after World War I.

CULTURE IN CONTEXT: Development in radio

Experiments with radio technology led to big advances in the early twentieth century, but it wasn't until about 1912 that the concept of **broadcasting** was realized. In 1916, the possibility of a radio broadcast receiver in every home was proposed.[10] Radio was increasingly used in World War I, but commercial broadcasting did not start until around 1920.[11]

The Printed Word

By 1900, new techniques for printing, binding, typesetting, and producing paper made the mass production of books, newspapers, and magazines possible. Mass production made the printed word more affordable and reading was an increasingly popular pastime, boosted by an increase in literacy rates.

Pulp magazines

There was a type of magazine called a pulp magazine that was named after the cheaper pulp paper on which it was printed. This pulp paper allowed the price of magazines to drop, making them more affordable. The first pulp magazine, called *The Golden Argosy*, was published in 1882 and was aimed at children. This magazine evolved into a new fiction magazine for adults, called *The Argosy*. It was nearly 200 pages long and packed with fiction and poetry. It became a great success. Pulp magazine publishers expanded and began to specialize in crime stories, westerns, romances, adventures, and fantasies with magazines such as *Detective Story Magazine* and *New Buffalo Bill Weekly*.

Miscellany periodicals

One of the most popular forms of magazine was the **miscellany** periodical. These magazines were a combination of short stories and articles on travel, political events, and technological oddities. They provided people who could not afford to travel the opportunity to read and learn about places near and far. They also supplied those with even the smallest sum of disposable income with ideas for entertainment. These periodicals popularized short stories such as Sir Arthur Conan Doyle's Sherlock Holmes mysteries (see pages 32–33). Unlike serial stories, these short stories didn't require any previous knowledge on the part of the reader. They were also just the right length for the commute that people were making on the new subway trains.

The dime novel

In the United States dime novels were popular until about 1915. These were usually inexpensive paperbacks containing adventure fiction, usually with a western theme or a science fiction element.[1]

COMPLETE NEW SHERLOCK HOLMES STORY
The Adventure of the Sussex Vampire

THE
STRAND
MAGAZINE

A TIP
FOR THE
TONGUE
SEE
PAGE 6

ALSO
CONAN DOYLE
ON
SHERLOCK HOLMES
IN HIS REMINISCENCES

Short stories featuring the detective Sherlock Holmes were popular in miscellany periodicals.

Women's magazines

Looking at a news agent's magazine shelf today you might be surprised to learn that many of today's women's magazines were being published in the early twentieth century. For example, *Good Housekeeping* was founded in 1885, *Vogue* was founded in 1892, *Harper's Bazaar* in 1867, and *Vanity Fair* first appeared in 1859 and was reintroduced in 1914.[2] The 1914 version of *Vanity Fair* was a cultural force during the Jazz Age, because it published the work of modern artists, illustrators, and writers.[3]

Vogue was originally intended to be a weekly high-society journal for New York City's social elite. However, when Condé Nast bought it in 1909 he transformed it into an influential women's fashion magazine focused on beauty, conduct, and etiquette.

Condé Nast became the first person to publish international editions of magazines when he published a British *Vogue* in 1916.[4]

Condé Nast (1873-1942)

Condé Nast and his company had a worldwide influence on popular culture. Nast built on the success of *Vogue* by buying other magazines, such as *Vanity Fair* and *House & Garden*. His innovative publishing theory was the concept of specialized publishing. This is when a publication is aimed at a particular group of people who share common interests. By aiming these magazines at certain specialized groups, Nast created magazines that were sophisticated and glamorous and influential on fashionable trends.

Comics

What we think of as the comic strip developed in the United States. But before this, European newspapers, magazines, and books published stories in cartoon form. Swiss artist Rodolphe Töpffer divided his picture stories into frames and added narrative to each frame. Picture stories with the title characters of such comic strips as *Max und Moritz* and *Ally Sloper* became popular in Germany and England.[5]

In the United States comics grew in popularity between 1895 and 1905,[6] when the comic strip was used in newspaper **circulation wars**. Improvements in color printing led to the introduction of **color supplements** in U.S. Sunday papers. These Sunday supplements featured comic strips. There was such a big demand from readers for these comics that by 1910 newspapers were publishing small books that contained previously published comic strips.[7]

Artist Richard Felton Outcault is credited with creating the first newspaper comic strip in the United States, called *The Yellow Kid*, in 1896.[8] Many other artists turned their attention to the comic strip. Rudolph Dirks was the first person to create what we now recognize as a comic strip with speech balloons and cartoon panels. His strip *The Katzenjammer Kids* appeared in the *Journal American* on December 12, 1897.[9]

The first successful daily newspaper comic strip was created in 1907 by Bud Fisher. *Mutt and Jeff* went on to be a favorite with U.S. audiences for decades. There has even been sheet music created based on the *Mutt and Jeff* characters!

Literature

People interested in literature were reading work by authors such as Virginia Woolf, E. M. Forster, James Joyce, Somerset Maugham, D. H. Lawrence, Henry James, and Mark Twain.

New types of fiction were becoming popular in these decades. The mainstream fiction of the **Victorian era** was typically a three-volume novel about domestic life. The popularity of these was replaced with the more accessible single-volume, faster-paced literature, such as adventure and detective stories and the science fiction novel.[10]

Science fiction

Science fiction was a popular **genre** of novels during these decades. The novels of author H. G. Wells shaped the way many people thought and behaved. Wells's science fiction novels contained predictions of air combat, contact between planets, and eugenics—the practice of altering a population by controlled breeding. Examples of his science fiction work include *The War of the Worlds* (1898), *The War in the Air* (1908), and *The First Men in the Moon* (1901).[11] Wells also wrote popular comic novels, including *Kipps* (1905) and *The History of Mr. Polly* (1910),[12] about how the lower middle class lived.

Adventure stories

Adventure stories, such as Rudyard Kipling's *The Jungle Book* (1894) and *Just So Stories* (1902), added a bit of excitement to life and kept the reader gripped. In 1907, Kipling was awarded the Nobel Prize for Literature, becoming the first writer in English to receive it.[13] Kipling wrote about India at the height of the British Empire. His stories were often romantic and sentimental. Another English writer known for his adventure novels was Henry Rider Haggard. Many of his stories were set in Africa. He is best known for his books *King Solomon's Mines* (1885) and *She* (1889).[14]

Detective novels

The detective novel was a new form of fiction. Detective stories became popular in magazines in the late nineteenth century but didn't become popular as novels until the twentieth century. Then they took off in a big way.[15] Sir Arthur Conan Doyle's famous detective, Sherlock Holmes, first appeared in 1887 but remained popular for decades to come. There was such an outcry from the public when Conan Doyle killed off Holmes that he had to resurrect this popular character in *The Hound of the Baskervilles* published in 1902.[16]

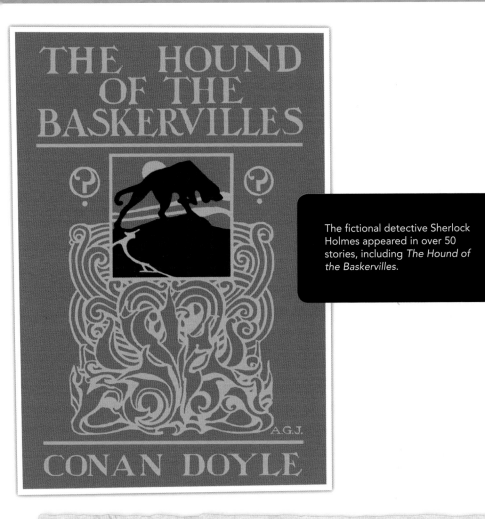

The fictional detective Sherlock Holmes appeared in over 50 stories, including *The Hound of the Baskervilles*.

Fan magazines

Fan magazines first appeared in 1911. *Motion Picture Story Magazine* was launched in the United States with the intention of advertising movies. It provided short pieces of fiction to promote the important movies of one of the major film companies, Vitagraph. In the United Kingdom, *The Pictures* used a similar approach. People liked these magazines because they felt that they were getting privileged information. The short stories also helped movie goers understand what was happening in the films since there was no spoken dialogue in the early motion pictures.

Wartime literature

World War I affected all areas of people's lives. The tragic, brutal events that occurred made some people want to write about their experiences. Sometimes people weren't able to do this, though, until some time had elapsed since the war. Other people whose lives had also been dominated by the war wanted to read these works.

Poetry

Poetry is a popular way of expressing feelings. Siegfried Sassoon was an English poet and writer who wrote poetry about the stark reality of war while he was serving in the British Army. He wrote about his compassion for his fellow soldiers as well as his contempt for the war leaders and what he thought was their insincere patriotic talk. While Sassoon was hospitalized in 1917[17] he met the poet Wilfred Owen. Sassoon gave Owen encouragement to write about the war. Owen's poems are about the horrors of war and his pity for the victims. Sadly, Owen became one of these victims when he was killed in 1918 during the final days of battle. Only five of Owen's poems were published during his lifetime, but his reputation grew when Sassoon published Owen's work in 1920. Owen's most famous work includes "Strange Meeting" and "Anthem for Doomed Youth."[18]

The Canadian John McCrae wrote the famous poem "In Flanders Fields." It is from this poem that poppies have become associated with World War I. In it McCrae writes of poppies blowing between the crosses that act as gravestones. Paper poppies are now sold in many countries to raise money for war veterans and people wear them to show their remembrance of those who died in World War I and World War II.

This portrait of Wilfred Owen was taken about 1916.

Prose

Some people wrote about their wartime experiences in the forms of memoirs and diaries. *Le Feu* (*Under Fire*) (1917)[19] by Henri Barbusse is a firsthand account of the life of French soldiers. Robert Graves wrote a memoir titled *Good-bye to All That* (1929).[20] Others used World War I as the setting for their novels, including Erich Maria Remarque with *All Quiet on the Western Front* (1929).[21] A film version of this successful novel is often shown on TV today. Rebecca West's *The Return of the Soldier* (1918)[22] is about life on the **home front**, and John Dos Passos's *Three Soldiers* (1921) is based on his experience as an ambulance driver during the war.

British soldiers climb over the tops of the trenches during the Battle of the Somme in 1916. The horrors faced in the trenches led some people to write about their experiences.

World War I songs

World War I inspired many songs. Some of them were about the war, others were written to keep up morale. Popular songs of the time included:

- "It's a Long Way to Tipperary"
- "Oh! It's a Lovely War"
- "Over There"
- "Pack Up Your Troubles in Your Old Kit Bag"

Art and Design

If you were to look up which artists were working between 1900 and 1919, you would find some famous names. Pablo Picasso and Georges Braque were inventing **cubism**. Wassily Kandinsky was painting early abstract art. Henri Matisse was experimenting with color. Marcel Duchamp was shocking the art world with his ready-made piece called *Fountain*, which was just a urinal signed "R. Mutt." The **surrealists**, such as Salvador Dalí and René Magritte, were forming and experimenting with the link between reality and dreams. But the ordinary person in the years from 1900 to 1919 would probably not have even heard of these artists. Until the 1960s with the rise of pop art, art was not accessible to the general public. Only a few wealthy individuals were able to afford to buy art. However, what the artists were doing played a significant role in the look and style of the era.

Art nouveau

At the end of the nineteenth century and early twentieth century, artists and designers wanted a new art that reflected the new materials they were using. Under the term *art nouveau*, or "new art," artists, architects, and designers experimented with new materials and techniques. The style they created was ornamental and inspired by nature. It used long, flowing lines and natural curves.

The poster

Art nouveau and the poster went well together. The poster was a piece of art that could look beautiful in addition to being useful by advertising products or events. The poster had a big impact on history, too. During World War I it was the most important of all visual media. It could be printed quickly and put up where the public could see it to have an immediate impact. A poster could also communicate with people who couldn't read (see pages 42–43).

Depending on where they lived, the public would have seen this art form all around them. Art nouveau was used for architecture, interior design, jewelry and glass design, posters, and illustration. In the United States, the art nouveau style appeared in the work of popular artist Louis Comfort Tiffany. By 1900, Tiffany was creating lamps, jewelry, and pottery as well as his celebrated glasswork. His work made him a leader of the art nouveau movement. In London, the shop Liberty & Company was very influential in promoting the style. Liberty sold carpets and furniture in the art nouveau style, and also designed art nouveau fabrics used for clothing and furnishings. This was the fashionable place to shop.

In France, Hector Guimard designed the signs for the Paris Metro in the art nouveau style.

Architecture and design

While art nouveau remained popular up until World War I, there was a group of architects who started a new way of thinking about design. Their style was called **modernism**. These architects wanted to clear away fussy style and ornament and look at design in terms of function. They wanted to strip a design back to the basics and consider, for example, what a building needed to do and what materials were needed to achieve this. The new approach of modernism was being used all over the world, but was easiest in the United States because there weren't centuries of tradition to overcome. Architects began to question why they should build an exciting new skyscraper and then cover it with decorations from an old pattern book.

One of the most successful architects of this new approach was American Frank Lloyd Wright, who designed buildings such as 540 Fair Oaks Avenue in Oak Park, Illinois, in 1902. Wright was the leading figure in what became known as the Prairie School of architecture.[1] Wright's prairie-style houses revolutionized the design of American homes. These houses had long, low, horizontal lines and intercommunicating interior spaces appealing to the way people wanted to live at the time. Wright's concept of "organic architecture" influenced architects throughout the United States and the world.

Frank Lloyd Wright's Robie House in Chicago, Illinois, shown around 1915. You can see the strong horizontal lines that made his designs so striking.

The Bauhaus teachers. From left to right: Albers, Scheper, Muche, Moholy- Nagy, Bayer, Schmidt, Gropius, Breuer, Kandinsky, Klee, Feininger, Stolzl, and Schlemmer.

Bauhaus

Bauhaus is the name of a school of architecture in Dessau, Germany, that was founded by Walter Gropius in 1919.[2] The school wanted to prove that art and engineering could work together instead of separately as previously thought. The Bauhaus ideals involved machine production as part of the design. The Bauhaus philosophy was that a building or object should be designed around the technology of mass production. This would allow objects to be made for the masses, rather than just for wealthy individuals.

Before students were allowed entry to the school, they had to take a six-month course. They were taught by some of the most outstanding artists of the twentieth century, including Josef Albers, Laszlo Moholy-Nagy, Paul Klee, Wassily Kandinsky, and Ludwig Mies van der Rohe.[3] The students were involved in the design of a Bauhaus building and all its fixtures and fittings. The Bauhaus style has influenced design beyond architecture, such as furniture and other objects for the home.

Notable architecture of the decades

1904: Frank Lloyd Wright, Larkin Building
1907–1909: Frank Lloyd Wright, Robie House
1909–1912: Peter Behrens, AEG Factory
1911–1914: Walter Gropius & Adolf Meyer, Fagus Works

Photography

The first photograph was taken in 1826. By 1900, photography was no longer a new invention, and people were exploring the possibilities that photography offered them. Mass-market photography had been available since 1889, when the first Kodak camera with a flexible roll of film was launched with the slogan "You push the button, we do the rest."[4] Photography became a popular pastime.

Did you know?

Between 1900 and 1919 color photography was still not available. The first color film was introduced in 1935 by Eastman Kodak Company.[5]

Photography as an art form

Photographers were starting to compose their shots as an artist would compose a painting. Initially photography wasn't regarded as an art form in the way that a painting or drawing was. This was because the camera seemed to do the work. Some people argued that the photographer didn't require imagination, creativity, or the manual skills that an artist did. The interest in photography grew, and the photo gradually became accepted as an art form. Art dealers and photographers, such as the American Alfred Stieglitz, started to promote photography as an art form and held exhibitions of photographers' work.[6]

Documentary photography

Photography could be more than just a hobby or a form of artwork. Starting in the late nineteenth century, many photographers were using photos to influence society and culture by highlighting social problems. Jacob A. Riis, a Danish immigrant to the United States, used his camera to document the poverty faced by the urban poor.[7] Lewis Hine published his photos of the immigrants of Ellis Island, New York, in 1908. He was hired by the National Child Labor Committee in 1911 to record the child labor abuses in order to bring about a change in the law.[8]

Lewis Hine took this photo of child laborers working in beet fields in Colorado in 1915.

Cameras on the front line

During World War I, the new, smaller, lightweight cameras were used by some soldiers to take photos of the fighting, even though they were ordered not to. The best of these shots from the front line were published in daily newspapers. The soldiers who took these photos were taking big risks to obtain the most spectacular or frightening photographs. They put themselves in physical danger on the battle scene and also risked facing a firing squad if they were caught taking the photos.[9]

Wartime Propaganda

What is propaganda? Propaganda is an organized program of publicity to promote particular beliefs. Before the twentieth century, the term had a neutral meaning. Since World War I, however, the term has a more sinister, manipulative implication. During World War I, governments needed a different way to influence the public. New military technology, such as machine guns, meant that soldiers were being killed in large numbers, and traditional forms of recruitment weren't enough. Governments needed to find a different way to sway public opinion. The answer was in the relatively new forms of mass communication. Cheap newspapers, posters, and movies meant the government could communicate on a daily basis.

Propaganda posters and movies

Governments made wartime propaganda look familiar by designing it like movie posters and advertisements (see pages 36–37). They also made it look glamorous by exploiting the images of fantasy and desire created by mass entertainment. Propaganda movies were made like westerns or crime dramas, and used popular personalities from movies, music, and sports. For example, Charlie Chaplin made *The Bond*, a propaganda movie to promote U.S. Liberty Bonds during World War I.[1] They even used cartoon characters to spread the official messages of the war effort.

The U.S. Army's iconic 1917 recruitment poster uses the image of Uncle Sam to deliver the message, rather than a real solider or recognizable politician. This poster was designed by James Montgomery Flagg.

Recruitment posters were made to look like advertisements and movie posters. Before World War I, few people would have considered joining the army. But posters with messages such as "I Want You for the U.S. Army" and "Your Country Needs You" brought world events to the general public's attention and encouraged people to become heroes.

Newsreels

Newsreels were a common part of the movie experience. They would be shown before the start of the feature film. During the war, newsreels were carefully censored by the government to ensure that only the information the government wanted the public to know would be shown. Some films even mixed genuine news footage with fictional sequences, such as D. W. Griffith's *Hearts of the World* (1918).[2]

This British recruitment poster was designed in 1914 by Alfred Leete. In this poster he made Secretary of State for War Lord Kitchener into an iconic image.

Pathé Newsreels

The weekly Pathé newsreels dominated the world market in the early 1900s, and by 1908 Charles Pathé's company (see page 14) was the world's largest film producer. The French-based company was selling twice as many films in the United States as all the U.S. film companies combined. The Pathé network collapsed with the outbreak of war, but the governments involved in the war quickly produced their own newsreels. These newsreels showed a biased version of world events.[3]

Fashion

There were many ways in which fashion influenced popular culture, and ways in which popular culture influenced fashion. People wanted to copy the glamour of the movie stars that they saw at the movie theater and in their magazines. These stars appeared with flawless makeup, and women wanted this look, too. The automobile craze influenced what people wore. The bicycle affected fashion, too—especially ladies' fashion, because women needed clothing they could pedal in safely. The increase in leisure time meant that sportswear and bathing suits were in demand. The women's rights movement influenced fashion as women fought for equality.

Fashion at the turn of the century

At the turn of the century it was common for women to wear uncomfortable and complicated clothes, such as corsets. Corsets are undergarments that pull in the waist and support the bosom. They were incredibly uncomfortable to wear and restricted the movement and breathing of the wearer. Corsets were used to give the body a different shape that was viewed as appealing by society at the time.

French designers Paul Poiret and Madeleine Vionnet are given the credit for liberating women from uncomfortable corsets.[1] Poiret's early dress designs were simple and straight. A corset would have changed the shape of these designs so he opted for the brassiere. Madeleine Vionnet created fluid, flowing designs that included new shapes such as cowl and halter necklines.

Menswear

Fashionable men wore pants, a waistcoat, and a coat with a top hat. After 1880, the trend for beards passed and men were clean-shaven or wore just a mustache.[2]

Sportswear

The trend for sportswear was just beginning at the turn of the century, as clothing started to be made for the increasingly active women who took part in sports such as tennis, horse riding, sailing, and archery. Sportswear consisted of informal separates such as blouses, shirts, skirts, and shorts.

Women were expected to dress modestly, so their clothing had high necklines and skirts that reached the ground.

Swimsuits

The acceptance of more relaxed clothing for sports affected swimwear. Today we think of swimwear as being swim shorts or trunks for men, and swimsuits or bikinis for women. However, early swimsuits covered most of the body so the wearer maintained modesty. For people wanting to go for a dip in the water, bathing was strictly segregated. By the early twentieth century, men started to wear shorts without a top. In 1900,[3] Australian swimmer and movie star Annette Kellerman introduced a loose one-piece swimsuit. It was made of wool! Just imagine how uncomfortable it must have been, especially when wet!

Bathers on the beach near Atlantic City, New Jersey, show off the latest swimsuit fashions.

Did you know?

It became acceptable to wear lipstick in public around 1912.

Hair and makeup

Women wanted to look like their favorite movie stars, so the demand for cosmetics increased. Familiar names in the beauty industry include Max Factor, Maybelline, and L'Oréal. These companies all started out in the 1900s. Max Factor was a Polish immigrant who moved to Los Angeles and started to sell makeup that didn't crack or cake to movie stars. In 1910, French chemist Eugene Schueller founded L'Oréal, which provided the first safe commercial hair dye. In 1914, T. J. Williams founded Maybelline, a cosmetics company that specialized in mascara. A year later, in 1915, Maurice Levy invented a metal container for lipstick.[7] Women were then able to easily carry their lipstick around with them in their handbags.

Did you know?

The zipper was launched in 1914 by Swedish-born engineer Gideon Sundback.[8] Sundback's zipper was used by the U.S. Army on the clothing and gear of World War I troops.[9]

Bicycles and freedom

The development in the late 1880s of the safety bicycle, which looked more like today's standard bicycle, also affected women's fashion. Some women started to wear a kind of pants to ride their bicycles. In the 1850s, American journalist Amelia Jenks Bloomer recommended wearing an outfit that consisted of a short jacket, a skirt, and loose pants that gathered at the ankles. The look didn't take off and Bloomer was mocked. However, the name "bloomers" survived and was used to describe the divided skirts women used for cycling.[4]

In addition to changing women's fashion in the 1900s, the bicycle also helped with the fight for women's equality. The bicycle gave women more personal freedom. It was adopted as a symbol of freedom by the suffragette movement.[5] Susan B. Anthony, a leader of the U.S. suffragette movement, declared that the bicycle did more than anything else did to **emancipate** women.[6]

Wartime fashion

World War I had an effect on every area of people's lives, even on fashion. Fashion became practical. The fashion for women's skirts before the war was ankle-length, but the hemline of skirts jumped to mid-calf by 1916.[10] The narrow hobble skirts that were introduced by Poiret were discarded in favor of more practical, wider skirts. Pants for women had been thought ugly but were seen as practical for war work. Short hair was seen as a sensible safety measure for women working in factories.

Uniforms

Women involved in the war effort and those who had joined military organizations wore uniforms. These military uniforms influenced the shape of fashionable dress.

CULTURE IN CONTEXT: War shortages

During the war there were shortages of many important things, such as food and building materials. There was also a shortage of fabric and fabric dye. This meant that fashions used less material than they did before the war. The shortage of dye meant that the colors available in the fashion world were limited.

Relaxation of rules

Up until World War I, there had been many rules for how men and women dressed. These rules had been in place since the more formal Victorian era.[11] The impact of war meant that these rules were relaxed. Ostentatious fashion didn't seem so important when families of all classes were losing sons and brothers in mud-filled trenches.

With their new shorter skirt lengths, women wore heeled shoes and skin-colored stockings, not the high-button boots of earlier days. The war also spelled the end of the corset. With the practical work women were doing, such as nursing, factory work, and ambulance driving, corsets were too awkward and impractical. Women were discouraged from buying corsets made with steel, which would go to better use in war equipment. This saved 28,000 tons of steel in 1917—enough to build two battleships![12]

After the war

After World War I ended in 1918, fashions changed again to a more informal look. There was a new enthusiasm for fashion. Underwear continued to be simplified once the corset was no longer worn. Women were trying to achieve a more girlish, straight silhouette. For relaxed, everyday clothing, sportswear was becoming very popular, especially in the United States. French designer Coco Chanel was having success with her "total look." She was the first designer to work skillfully with wool jersey fabric. This material was originally intended to make men's sports clothes, but she used it to make comfortable, chic clothes.[13]

During the war, fashions became simpler and more practical.

Changing Times

The great technological advances made at the start of the twentieth century changed society. The affordable car had a huge impact on where people could live and gave them the freedom to travel where they wanted to. Mass production of products such as cars, clothes, and magazines meant that they became more affordable. Time-saving devices such as the first electric washing machine meant people had more leisure time—more time for spending at the movies or dancing the cakewalk!

The age of imperialism was at an end, and people were viewing the United States as the exciting place to be. All things American became popular.

The demand for equality for women and for people of color was growing. Women finally got the right to vote in the United Kingdom in 1918 and in the United States in 1920.[1] The racial divide between blacks and whites continued from 1900 to 1919, but African American culture, especially in the United States, was influencing the trends of white society. For example, ragtime and jazz music and dances became more mainstream.

Overshadowed by war

The period from 1900 to 1919 was overshadowed by World War I. This war was supposed to be the war that ended all wars. Yet World War II occurred only 20 years later. The new technology that was so exciting in civilian life was devastating in the military world. The airplane, combined with the new machine guns and bombs, increased the fighting in the skies and over enemy territory. Technology changed the face of war and made it more brutal and deadly.

War also affected people on the home front. Everyone became part of the war effort and it changed their lives. Fashion seemed trivial compared with the realities of war. People wanted to know what was going on at the war front, so newspapers, newsreels, magazines, poetry, and fiction about the war were popular. But people also looked for escapism, and the new motion pictures were a great place to find this (see pages 14-19). A whole industry developed around the glamour of the film.

New technologies such as tanks and machine guns changed the nature of modern warfare.

What Did the 1900s and 1910s Do for Us?

The 1900s and 1910s are influential in today's popular culture. The technology may have advanced, but motion pictures and photography still play a key role in today's leisure activities. Film production companies that were set up in the 1900s and 1910s, such as Universal Pictures and what became known as MGM, are still influential today. Although it is no longer the world's center for film production, Hollywood is still associated with the greats of film, and many film stars live in neighboring communities. The star system is still an established part of the film industry, and the public and media have an obsession with the latest film stars.

Jazz quickly developed and changed over the following decades, and still lives on in its many forms to delight audiences around the world. The technologies of sound recording have advanced to the degree that we are now able to hear original jazz recordings in a new, improved, digitally remastered form.

This postcard from 1911 shows the Titanic before setting off on its fateful journey across the Atlantic in April 1912.

In 2009, an exhibition was held to celebrate the 90th anniversary of the Bauhaus movement, which influenced modern art, design, and architecture.

Today's fashion enthusiasts are still being instructed by *Vogue* as to what to wear, what exhibitions to attend, and how to live stylishly, although perhaps they are reading it all online. It's hard to imagine today's women and girls not having the choice of wearing pants. And where would we be without the zipper? Early twentieth century designers still influence today's fashions as designers continually recycle and reuse "vintage" looks. French designer Paul Poiret was the first designer to introduce the concept of "designer" perfume to complement the lifestyle created by his fashions. Nowadays it's rare to find a designer who doesn't have at least one perfume to offer customers.

Bauhaus design and architecture still look modern today, as does prairie style. It's hard to believe that some of it is nearly 100 years old. The art of this period is still fashionable, although it is more likely today's homes might have a poster or a print by an avant-garde artist such as Picasso or Matisse, who were unknown to the general public in the early 1900s. Today's shops stock furniture and other objects designed by some of the greats of this era, including modernist Mies van der Rohe. In cities around the world, the architecture of this period can still be seen. Mies van der Rohe, for example, was responsible for much of Chicago's skyline.

Even the disasters from this period still affect people today. The sinking of *Titanic*, and the stories and legends that surround it, fascinated the public at the time and continue to do so 100 years later. In May 2011, the cigar box of the captain of *Titanic* sold for £250,000[1] (over $393,000) and the plans used to investigate the sinking of the *Titanic* reached £220,000[2] (over $346,000).

Timeline

1901
Queen Victoria dies and is succeeded by Edward VII.

September 1901
President McKinley shot by anarchist. Theodore Roosevelt becomes president.

1901
Australian Immigration Restriction Act of 1901 limits immigration to Australia to mostly Europeans. British emigrants are encouraged by the offer of land.

1902
Beatrix Potter's *The Tale of Peter Rabbit* is published.

December 1903
The Wright brothers make the first successful flight.

1904
London's first electric underground train is in service.

1904
New York City's subway system is opened.

1905
The first movie theater opens in Pittsburgh, Pennsylvania.

1905
Albert Einstein's Special Theory of Relativity is published.

1906
First animated cartoon, *Humorous Phases of Funny Faces*, is produced.

1907
Ziegfeld Follies begin performing.

1907
First successful daily comic strip, *Mutt and Jeff*, is published.

1908
Ford Model T car is released.

1908
The tea bag is introduced.

1908
The Boy Scout movement is founded.

1909
General Electric (GE) patents and produces the electric toaster.

1909
Vogue bought by Condé Nast and transformed into an influential women's magazine.

1911
Fan magazines first appear.

April 1912
Titanic sinks.

1912
First blues record published.

1913
Henry Ford opens the first moving assembly line in Michigan.

June 28, 1914
Archduke Franz Ferdinand is **assassinated**.

August 9, 1914
Britain declares war on Germany in response to the invasion of Belgium.

1914
Vanity Fair is relaunched.

1915
78 rpm record is available.

September 15, 1916
Tanks are used by the British for the first time at Flers, France.

1917
First jazz recordings made.

April 1917
United States enters World War I.

November 7, 1917
Communist revolution begins in Russia.

November 11, 1918
World War I ends.

June 14–15, 1919
First nonstop flight made across the Atlantic Ocean.

1919
Felix the Cat is created.

Best of the Era

The best way to find out about the pop culture of the 1900s and 1910s is to experience it for yourself. Here are some suggestions for the best or most typical examples that will give you a sense of the time.

Movies

Cinderella
The Great Train Robbery
The Life of an American Fireman
Quo Vadis
Voyage to the Moon

Music

King of Ragtime by Scott Joplin
King Oliver by Oliver's Creole Jazz Band
The Library of Congress Recordings by Jelly Roll Morton

Literature

Arthur Conan Doyle: *The Hound of the Baskervilles*
John Dos Passos: *Three Soldiers*
Robert Graves: *Over the Brazier* and *Fairies and Fusiliers*
Erich Maria Remarque: *All Quiet on the Western Front*
H. G. Wells:
      The First Men in the Moon
      The War of the Worlds
Rebecca West: *The Return of the Soldier*
Oscar Wilde: *The Picture of Dorian Gray*

Drama & Theater

J. M. Barrie: *The Admirable Crichton* and *Peter Pan*
Oscar Wilde: *Lady Windermere's Fan* and *The Importance of Being Earnest*

Architecture

Behrens: AEG Factory
Gropius & Meyer: Fagus Works
Wright: Larkin Building and Robie House

Notes on Sources

What Is Popular Culture?

1. *The Oxford English Reference Dictionary*, Oxford University Press, 1996, 264.

2. s.v. "World War I," *Britannica Student Encyclopedia, Encyclopedia Britannica Online Library Edition, Encyclopædia Britannica*, 2011, http://library.eb.co.uk/all/comptons/article-9277797, Accessed June 2, 2011.

3. s.v. "woman suffrage," *Encyclopædia Britannica, Encyclopædia Britannica Online Library Edition, Encyclopædia Britannica*, 2011, http://library.eb.co.uk/eb/article-284442, Accessed April 19, 2011.

4. Joanna Hunter, *A Century in Photographs*, London: Times Newspapers, Ltd.,1999, 41.

5. http://www.localhistories.org/20thcent.html, Accessed July 17, 2011.

6. http://www.jazzistry.org/timeline.html, Accessed July 17, 2011.

7. s.v. "subway," *Encyclopædia Britannica, Encyclopædia Britannica Online Library Edition,*

Encyclopædia Britannica, 2011, http://library.eb.co.uk/eb/article-9070117, Accessed June 3, 2011.

8. Hunter, *A Century in Photographs*, 23.

9. s.v. "subway," *Encyclopædia Britannica*.

10. s.v. "airplane," *Britannica Student Encyclopedia, Encyclopædia Britannica Online Library Edition, Encyclopædia Britannica*, 2011, http://library.eb.co.uk/all/comptons/article-230877, Accessed June 3, 2011.

11. *The Oxford English Reference Dictionary*, 31.

12. Hunter, *A Century in Photographs*, 21.

13. Hunter, *A Century in Photographs*, 41.

14. s.v. "automobile," *Encyclopædia Britannica, Encyclopædia Britannica Online Library Edition, Encyclopædia Britannica*, 2011, http://library.eb.co.uk/eb/article-259068, Accessed July 18, 2011.

15. Hunter, *A Century in Photographs*, 41.

16. s.v. "United States." *Encyclopædia Britannica, Encyclopædia Britannica Online Library Edition, Encyclopædia Britannica*, Inc., 2011, http://library.eb.co.uk/eb/article-78004, Accessed July 18, 2011.

17. Immigration to United States, Video, *Encyclopedia Britannica Online Library Edition*, http://library.eb.co.uk/eb/art-71911, Accessed July 18, 2011.

Children's Entertainment

1. "jigsaw puzzle," *Encyclopædia Britannica, Encyclopædia Britannica Online Library Edition, Encyclopædia Britannica*, 2011, http://library.eb.co.uk/eb/article-9043634, Accessed April 12, 2011.

2. s.v. "Roosevelt, Theodore," *Encyclopædia Britannica, Encyclopedia Britannica Online Library Edition, Encyclopædia Britannica*, 2011, http://library.eb.co.uk/eb/article-8428, Accessed June 2, 2011.

3. http://ezinearticles.com/?Toys-in-the-Early-

1900s&id=2142431, Accessed April 12, 2011.

4. http://www.meccano.com/about/history/, Accessed June 1, 2011.

5. s.v. "child labor," *Britannica Student Encyclopedia, Encyclopedia Britannica Online Library Edition, Encyclopædia Britannica*, 2011, http://library.eb.co.uk/all/comptons/article-234147, Accessed June 1, 2011.

6. http://www.educationbug.org/a/compulsory-education.html, Accessed July 18, 2011.

Film and Light Entertainment

1. http://www.factmonster.com/ce6/ent/A0859791.html, Accessed April 12, 2011.

2. s.v. "motion picture, history of the," *Encyclopædia Britannica, Encyclopedia Britannica Online Library Edition, Encyclopædia Britannica*, 2011, http://library.eb.co.uk/eb/article-52138, Accessed May 31, 2011.

3. s.v. "motion picture, history of the," *Encyclopædia Britannica*.

4. s.v. "motion picture, history of the," *Encyclopædia Britannica*.

5. s.v. "Porter, Edwin S.," *Encyclopædia Britannica, Encyclopedia Britannica Online Library Edition, Encyclopædia Britannica*, 2011, http://library.eb.co.uk/eb/article-9060965, Accessed May 31, 2011.

6. s.v. "Birth of a Nation, The," *Encyclopædia Britannica, Encyclopedia Britannica Online Library Edition, Encyclopædia Britannica*, 2011, http://library.eb.co.uk/eb/article-9477268, Accessed May 31, 2011.

7. s.v. "Birth of a Nation, The," *Encyclopædia Britannica*.

8. s.v. "Griffith, D(avid) W(ark)," *Encyclopædia Britannica, Encyclopedia Britannica Online Library Edition, Encyclopædia Britannica*, 2011, http://library.eb.co.uk/eb/article-2869, Accessed May 31, 2011.

9. s.v. "Porter, Edwin S.," *Encyclopædia Britannica*.

10. http://www.parliament.uk/documents/commons/lib/research/rp99/rp99-111.pdf, Accessed June 3, 2011.

11. s.v. "Laemmle, Carl," *Encyclopædia Britannica, Encyclopedia Britannica Online Library Edition, Encyclopædia Britannica*, 2011, http://library.eb.co.uk/eb/article-9472708, Accessed May 31, 2011.

12. s.v. "Pickford, Mary," *Encyclopædia Britannica, Encyclopedia Britannica Online Library Edition, Encyclopædia Britannica*, 2011, http://library.eb.co.uk/eb/article-9059931, Accessed June 2, 2011.

13. s.v. "Messmer, Otto," *Encyclopædia Britannica, Encyclopedia Britannica Online Library Edition, Encyclopædia Britannica*, 2011, http://library.eb.co.uk/eb/article-9106439, Accessed May 31, 2011.

14. s.v. "Ziegfeld, Florenz, Jr.," *Encyclopædia Britannica,* *Encyclopedia Britannica Online Library Edition,* Encyclopædia Britannica, 2011, http://library. eb.co.uk/eb/article-9078364, Accessed June 1, 2011.

15. s.v. "Fields, W.C.," *Britannica Student Encyclopedia,* *Encyclopedia Britannica Online Library Edition,* Encyclopædia Britannica, 2011, http://library. eb.co.uk/all/comptons/article-9274306, Accessed June 1, 2011.

16. s.v. "Keaton, Buster," *Encyclopædia Britannica,* *Encyclopedia Britannica Online Library Edition,* Encyclopædia Britannica, 2011, http://library.eb.co.uk/ eb/article-9044957, Accessed June 2, 2011.

17. s.v. "vaudeville," *Encyclopædia Britannica,* *Encyclopedia Britannica Online Library Edition,* Encyclopædia Britannica, 2011, http://library.eb.co.uk/ eb/article-9074912, Accessed June 1, 2011.

18. s.v. "Muni, Paul," *Encyclopædia Britannica,* *Encyclopædia Britannica Online Library Edition,* Encyclopædia Britannica, 2011, http://library.eb.co.uk/ eb/article-9054279, Accessed July 18, 2011.

19. s.v. "Metro-Goldwyn-Mayer, Inc.," *Britannica Student Encyclopedia, Encyclopædia Britannica Online Library Edition, Encyclopædia Britannica,* 2011, http://library.eb.co.uk/all/comptons/article-9312484, Accessed July 18, 2011.

Music

1. s.v. "ragtime," *Encyclopædia Britannica,* *Encyclopædia Britannica Online Library Edition,* Encyclopædia Britannica, 2011, 2011.http://library. eb.co.uk/eb/article-9062463, Accessed April 12, 2011.

2. Ian Carr, Digby Fairweather, and Brian Priestley, *The Rough Guide to Jazz,* London: Rough Guides Ltd., 1995, 742.

3. Carr, Fairweather, Priestley, *The Rough Guide to Jazz,* 742.

4. Carr, Fairweather, Priestley, *The Rough Guide to Jazz,* 345.

5. Carr, Fairweather, Priestley, *The Rough Guide to Jazz,* 344.

6. *The Oxford English Reference Dictionary,* 156.

7. s.v. "cakewalk," *Encyclopædia Britannica,* *Encyclopedia Britannica Online Library Edition,* Encyclopædia Britannica, 2011, http://library.eb.co.uk/ eb/article-9018592, Accessed May 31, 2011.

8. s.v. "dance, Western," *Encyclopædia Britannica,* *Encyclopedia Britannica Online Library Edition,* Encyclopædia Britannica, 2011, http://library.eb.co.uk/ eb/article-22138, Accessed July 18, 2011.

9. s.v. "phonograph," *Encyclopædia Britannica,* *Encyclopedia Britannica Online Library Edition,* Encyclopædia Britannica, 2011, http://library.eb.co.uk/ eb/article-9059766, Accessed May 31, 2011.

10. s.v. "radio," *Britannica Student Encyclopedia,* *Encyclopedia Britannica Online Library Edition,*

Encyclopædia Britannica, 2011, http://library.eb.co.uk/ all/comptons/article-207095, Accessed June 1, 2011.

11. s.v. "radio," *Britannica Student Encyclopedia,* http://library.eb.co.uk/all/comptons/article-286019, Accessed June 1, 2011.

The Printed Word

1. s.v. "dime novel," *Encyclopædia Britannica,* *Encyclopædia Britannica Online Library Edition,* Encyclopædia Britannica, 2011, http://library.eb.co.uk/ eb/article-9124824, Accessed July 18, 2011.

2. s.v. "Vanity Fair," *Encyclopædia Britannica,* *Encyclopedia Britannica Online Library Edition,* Encyclopædia Britannica, 2011, http://library.eb.co.uk/ eb/article-9471681, Accessed May 31, 2011.

3. s.v. "Vanity Fair," *Encyclopædia Britannica.*

4. http://www.referenceforbusiness.com/history2/54/ The-Cond-Nast-Publications-Inc.html, Accessed June 1, 2011.

5. s.v. "cartoons," *Britannica Student Encyclopedia,* *Encyclopædia Britannica Online Library Edition,* Encyclopædia Britannica, 2011, http://library.eb.co.uk/ all/comptons/article-198337, Accessed July 18, 2011.

6. http://www.enotes.com/1900-media-american-decades/sunday-color-comics, Accessed June 2, 2011.

7. http://www.enotes.com/how-products-encyclopedia/comic-book, Accessed June 2, 2011.

8. http://www.enotes.com/how-products-encyclopedia/comic-book, Accessed June 2, 2011.

9. http://www.comic-art.com/history/history1.htm, Accessed June 2, 2011.

10. Lee Server, *Encyclopedia of Pulp Fiction Writers,* Facts on File, 2002.

11. "1000 Makers of the Twentieth Century," London *Sunday Times,* 1991; s.v. "Wells, H. G.," *Encyclopædia Britannica, Encyclopedia Britannica Online Library Edition, Encyclopædia Britannica,* 2011, http://library. eb.co.uk/eb/article-7863, Accessed June 2, 2011.

12. s.v. "Wells, H. G.," *Encyclopædia Britannica.*

13. *The Oxford English Reference Dictionary,* 784.

14. *The Oxford English Reference Dictionary,* 632.

15. http://www.ucalgary.ca/applied_history/tutor/ popculture/, Accessed May 29, 2011.

16. http://www.ucalgary.ca/applied_history/tutor/ popculture/.

17. *The Oxford English Reference Dictionary,* 1286.

18. *The Oxford English Reference Dictionary,* 1040.

19. s.v. "Barbusse, Henri," *Encyclopædia Britannica,* *Encyclopedia Britannica Online Library Edition,* Encyclopædia Britannica, 2011, http://library.eb.co.uk/ eb/article-9013324, Accessed June 2, 2011.

20. s.v. "Graves, Robert," *Encyclopædia Britannica,* *Encyclopedia Britannica Online Library Edition,* Encyclopædia Britannica, 2011, http://library.eb.co.uk/

eb/article-9037784, Accessed June 2, 2011.

21. s.v. "Remarque, Erich Maria," *Encyclopædia Britannica, Encyclopedia Britannica Online Library Edition, Encyclopædia Britannica,* 2011,http://library.eb.co.uk/eb/article-9063148, Accessed June 2, 2011.

22. s.v. "West, Dame Rebecca," *Encyclopædia Britannica, Encyclopedia Britannica Online Library Edition, Encyclopædia Britannica,* 2011, http://library.eb.co.uk/eb/article-9076588, Accessed June 2, 2011.

Art and Design

1. s.v. "Wright, Frank Lloyd," *Encyclopædia Britannica, Encyclopædia Britannica Online Library Edition, Encyclopædia Britannica,* 2011, http://library.eb.co.uk/eb/article-8019, Accessed April 18, 2011.

2. *The Oxford English Reference Dictionary,* 121.

3. s.v. "Bauhaus," *Encyclopædia Britannica, Encyclopædia Britannica Online Library Edition, Encyclopædia Britannica,* 2011, http://library.eb.co.uk/eb/article-647, Accessed April 18, 2011; E. H. Gombrich, *The Story of Art,* London: Phaidon, 1989, 444.

4. s.v. "photography," *Britannica Student Encyclopedia, Encyclopedia Britannica Online Library Edition, Encyclopædia Britannica,* 2011, http://library.eb.co.uk/all/comptons/article-229823, Accessed June 2, 2011.

5. *The Oxford English Reference Dictionary,* 1092.

6. s.v. "photography," *Britannica Student Encyclopedia, Encyclopædia Britannica Online Library Edition, Encyclopædia Britannica,* 2011, http://library.eb.co.uk/all/comptons/article-206481, Accessed July 18, 2011.

7. s.v. "photography," *Britannica Student Encyclopedia,* http://library.eb.co.uk/all/comptons/article-229823, Accessed July 18, 2011.

8. s.v. "Hine, Lewis," *Britannica Student Encyclopedia, Encyclopædia Britannica Online Library Edition, Encyclopædia Britannica,* 2011, http://library.eb.co.uk/all/comptons/article-9311691, Accessed July 18, 2011.

9. http://www.art-ww1.com/gb/present.html, Accessed June 2, 2011.

Wartime Propaganda

1. http://www.imdb.com/title/tt0008907/, Accessed June 3, 2011.

2. Toby Clark, *Art and Propaganda,* London: George Weidenfeld and Nicolson, 1997, 104.

3. Clark, *Art and Propaganda,* 104.

Fashion

1. Bronwyn Cosgrave, *Costume and Fashion: A Complete History,* London: Hamlyn, 2003, 220.

2. s.v. "dress," *Encyclopædia Britannica, Encyclopædia Britannica Online Library Edition, Encyclopædia Britannica,* 2011, http://library.eb.co.uk/eb/article-14028, Accessed July 19, 2011.

3. s.v. "swimsuit," *Encyclopædia Britannica, Encyclopædia Britannica Online Library Edition, Encyclopædia Britannica,* 2011, http://library.eb.co.uk/eb/article-9070656, Accessed May 29, 2011.

4. s.v. "bloomers," *Encyclopædia Britannica, Encyclopædia Britannica Online Library Edition, Encyclopædia Britannica,* 2011, http://library.eb.co.uk/eb/article-9015718, Accessed May 29, 2011.

5. s.v. "bicycle," *Encyclopædia Britannica, Encyclopædia Britannica Online Library Edition, Encyclopædia Britannica,* 2011, http://library.eb.co.uk/eb/article-230025, Accessed May 29, 2011.

6. Sue Macy, *Wheels of Change: How Women Rode the Bicycle to Freedom* (With a Few Flat Tires Along the Way), Washington, D.C., National Geographic, 2011.

7. http://www.digitalhistory.uh.edu/do_history/fashion/Cosmetics/cosmetics.html, Accessed July 19, 2011.

8. Hunter, *A Century in Photographs,* 43.

9. http://www.invent.org/hall_of_fame/302.html, Accessed July 19, 2011.

10. http://www.costumes.org/classes/fashiondress/ww1toww2.htm, Accessed May 31, 2011.

11. http://www.costumes.org/classes/fashiondress/ww1toww2.htm.

12. http://muse.museum.montana.edu/sof/ww1.html, Accessed May 31, 2011.

13. s.v. "Chanel, Coco," *Encyclopædia Britannica, Encyclopædia Britannica Online Library Edition, Encyclopædia Britannica,* 2011, http://library.eb.co.uk/eb/article-9022401, Accessed April 19, 2011.

Changing Times

1. s.v. "suffrage," *Encyclopædia Britannica, Encyclopedia Britannica Online Library Edition, Encyclopædia Britannica,* 2011, http://library.eb.co.uk/eb/article-9070175, Accessed June 3, 2011.

What Did the 1900s and 1910s Do for Us?

1. http://www.bbc.co.uk/news/uk-england-merseyside-13450315, Accessed June 3, 2011.

2. http://www.bbc.co.uk/news/uk-england-wiltshire-13584306, Accessed June 3, 2011.

Find Out More

Books

Adams, Simon. *World War I*. New York: Dorling Kindersley, 2007.

Barber, Nicola. *World War I* (Living Through... series). Chicago: Heinemann Library, 2012.

Dixon-Engel, Tara, and Mike Jackson. *The Wright Brothers: First in Flight*. New York: Sterling, 2007.

Handyside, Christopher. *Jazz* (A History of American Music series). Chicago: Heinemann Library, 2006.

Jedicke, Peter. *Great Inventions of the 20th Century*. New York: Chelsea House Publishers, 2007.

Price, Sean. *Yanks in World War One* (Americans in the Trenches series). Chicago: Raintree, 2008.

Woodside, Martin. *Thomas Edison: The Man Who Lit Up the World*. New York: Sterling, 2007.

Websites

www.channel4.com/history/microsites/H/history/guide20/part09b.html
Read more about popular culture in the twentieth century.

kclibrary.lonestar.edu/decade00.html
Read more about American culture in the 1900s at this website.

kclibrary.lonestar.edu/decade10.html
Read more about American culture in the 1910s at this website.

muse.museum.montana.edu/sof/index.html
Explore fashion through time.

www.ww1photos.com/WW1MusicIndex.html
Hear the songs of World War I being sung.

tirocchi.stg.brown.edu/514/story/fashion_earlycentury.html
This website has lots of information about the changing fashions of the 1900s.

tirocchi.stg.brown.edu/514/story/fashion_teens.html
This website has lots of information about the changing fashions of the 1910s.

Topics for further research

- Investigate the fight for women's votes around the world.

- Research World War I in more detail to discover what lessons the world should learn from it and why it wasn't the "war to end all wars."

- Explore the world of twentieth century art and design. Who influenced whom?

Glossary

animation drawing, such as a cartoon, made to move

anti-Semitism against Jews

art nouveau popular, decorative style of design and art

assassinated killed

assembly line group of machines and workers to make (assemble) a product

axle center pin a wheel spins around on

broadcasting radio signals being sent from one location to a widespread audience

child labor children made to work

circulation war battle between newspapers over who can sell the most copies

color supplement magazine printed in color that comes with a newspaper

commercial flight flight that takes passengers for money

cubism art style utilizing geometric shapes and collages

dialogue conversation between two or more people

emancipate cause to be free

emigrant person who leaves one country to settle in another

empire number of countries ruled by one country

franchise freedom of women to vote

genre style

home front people at home during a war

honky-tonk style of piano playing in ragtime music

immigrant person who settles in another country

imperialism policy of extending a country's military power or cultural influence to other countries or places

improvised music that is played without preparation, without written down notes

miscellany mixture

modernism art style that broke with traditional styles and forms

pageantry elaborate parade

publicity stills still photographs used to promote a film or actor

record flat disk used to capture sounds

revue light entertainment made up of sketches, songs, and dances

risqué slightly indecent and liable to shock

rpm (revolutions per minute) how fast a record spins

suffragette woman protesting to get the right to vote

surrealism art style utilizing strange and dreamlike images

synchronized made to occur at the same time

title card screen shown between scenes in a film with writing to explain what is happening or provide dialogue

variety show show that includes acts by musicians, dancers, singers, and comedians

vaudeville show that includes acts by musicians, dancers, singers, and comedians. Vaudeville is another name for a variety show.

Victorian era era of Queen Victoria's reign

work song song sung, usually by a group, in time to the actions of work to prevent boredom during a repetitive task

World War I war between 1914 and 1918 that started between Austria-Hungary and Serbia and ended up involving most of the nations of the world

Index